The
Spelling Practice Workbook
7th Grade

Also by Natasha Attard, Ph.D.

The Spelling Practice Workbook for 6th Grade. Vocabulary Definitions, Model Sentences, Final Assessments. Guided Spelling Activities for the 6th Grade.

Vocabulary Building 7th Grade Workbook: Guided Activities to Increase your Word Power. Consolidates and Complements Homeschooling of the English Language

Vocabulary and Spelling Practice Grade 7: Intensive Practice Workbook and Guided Activities to Increase Your Word Power.

The Spelling Practice Workbook 8th Grade with Vocabulary Definitions, Model Sentences and Final Assessments: Guided Spelling Activities for 8th Grade.

The Spelling Practice Workbook

Guided Activities to Increase your Word Power

7th Grade

Natasha Attard Ph.D

First published 2023

ISBN 978-9918-0-0483-6 Paperback

To my boys, Giovanni and Beppe, with much love.

Contents

Contents

About this Book

This workbook integrates the learning of spelling and the meaning of words. While the main focus of this workbook is spelling accuracy, it also aims to enhance the student's retention of the words long-term, by teaching them to focus on both the definition and the spelling of each word. The structure of each lesson in this book is designed to facilitate this simultaneous learning.

This workbook contains 20 lessons, each lesson focusing on six words at a time, with each spelling activity centered on those words. Each word is accompanied by its definition and an example sentence, to enable the student to learn the meaning of the word as they practice spelling it. There are 120 words in total which the 7th grade student is expected to learn.

Each lesson begins with a drilling exercise of the words in syllables, allowing the student to practice spelling each part of the word correctly. After the syllable drilling exercise, the student moves on to another drilling exercise of the word in full, enabling them to practice spelling the word accurately and confidently.

To reinforce learning and retention, a word search puzzle is included, containing the target words for spelling, together with their synonyms. This exercise encourages the student to stay oriented on the meanings of the words they are studying, while also providing a fun and engaging way to reinforce their knowledge of the words.

Finally, a sentence composition exercise is included, to encourage the student to write their own sentence using the word. This exercise reinforces the meaning of each word, and gives the student an opportunity to practice both its spelling and its usage in context.

This workbook provides a comprehensive and engaging approach to spelling improvement, ensuring that the student not only learns how to spell each word accurately but also retains its meaning and usage in context.

How to Use this Book

Teachers and parents can use the workbook to supplement their regular spelling instruction or as a standalone resource. The structured approach, with 20 lessons and four practice exercises per lesson, makes it easy to integrate the workbook into any teaching or learning environment.

It is recommended that the student complete each lesson in sequence. Every lesson is designed to help the student improve their spelling accuracy and reinforce their understanding of the words' meanings.

To begin each lesson, the student should review the wordbank of six words and their definitions. Next, they should complete the drilling exercise of each word in syllables. Learning to spell words in syllables is a valuable skill that can improve accuracy, enhance knowledge retention, and build phonetic awareness. Breaking down complex words into smaller, more manageable parts helps the student to spell each syllable accurately, making it easier to remember the overall spelling of the word. The student should then complete the next drilling exercise of the word in full. This is followed by a word search puzzle which includes the six target words and their synonyms. This activity provides a fun and engaging way to reinforce learning and retention of the target words. Finally, the student should complete the sentence composition exercise, which reinforces the meaning of each word while giving them an opportunity to practice using the word in context.

To make it easier for teachers and parents who would like to focus on a specific lesson, the contents page of this workbook indicates the wordbank included in each lesson. It may also serve as a list for other language activities and for testing.

A Message from the Author

Dear Reader,

Thank you for choosing "The Spelling Practice Workbook for 7th Grade." As an educator and author, my deepest passion lies in guiding students through the intricacies of language. I am dedicated to helping each young learner overcome the hurdles they face in writing, particularly in spelling and vocabulary usage. It is my earnest belief that every student has the potential to excel in these areas, and it's my mission to unlock this potential through resources that are both educational and engaging.

To further support your child's academic journey, I'm excited to offer an exclusive, complimentary resource from my other publication, "Vocabulary and Spelling Practice for 7th Grade." This free online resource, accessible with your purchase, includes the first three lessons from "Vocabulary and Spelling Practice for 7th Grade." It's designed to align with the skills and knowledge your child is developing through "The Spelling Practice Workbook for 7th Grade."

What's Inside This Free Resource?

- **Guided Exercises**: Engaging activities that introduce vocabulary words, emphasizing their connotations and meanings in a way that's understandable and relatable for 7th graders.
- **Comprehensive Definitions:** Each word is accompanied by clear definitions and multiple example sentences, enhancing understanding through context.
- **Practical Application:** Diverse exercises for repeated practice, alongside spelling lessons that incorporate fun games. This approach ensures a deeper grasp of vocabulary and spelling.
- **Self-Assessment Tools:** At the end of the lesson, your child can test their knowledge, helping you track their progress and identify areas for improvement.

How to Access:

Scan the Code and it will take you to my website (natashascripts.com). Enter your name and email address and you will be redirected instantly to the free resource.

Warm regards,

Natasha Attard Ph.d

Lesson 1

Definitions

Adequate: enough or suitable for a particular purpose or situation.

Allocate: to divide or distribute resources, such as money or time, in a fair and organized way.

Indifferent: not having strong feelings one way or the other; having no preference.

Libel: writing or saying false things about someone that could harm their reputation.

Affiliation: a connection or relationship between two organizations or groups.

Condor: a large bird of prey found in the western United States and South America, known for its black feathers and long wingspan.

Example Sentences

I made sure to pack an **adequate** amount of snacks for the long car ride.

The school principal **allocated** the funds for the new playground equipment.

Although everyone else was excited about the trip, Ben was **indifferent** and didn't seem to care one way or the other.

Corvin was sued for **libel** after he wrote false and damaging information about his neighbor in a blog post.

The charity organization had an **affiliation** with a local church, which helped them reach more people in need.

The students learned about the endangered species, the California **condor**, and how they are trying to protect them.

Let's Practice Spelling the Word

eq **ua** adequate	ad - e - quate →	
ll allocate	al - lo - cate →	
in indifferent	in - dif - fer - ent →	
el libel	li - bel →	
ff **ia** affiliation	af - fil - i - a - tion →	
or condor	con - dor →	

Now write each word in full.

adequate	→	→
allocate	→	→
indifferent	→	→
libel	→	→
affiliation	→	→
condor	→	→

	→	
	→	
	→	
	→	
	→	
	→	

	→	
	→	
	→	
	→	
	→	
	→	

Puzzle 1

```
A  L  Q  C  O  N  D  O  R  W  I  K  L  A  Q
R  P  R  E  F  E  R  E  N  C  E  D  U  N  R
R  E  S  O  U  R  C  E  S  M  A  N  E  U  U
Q  G  P  C  O  G  K  W  R  Y  C  E  P  P  W
Q  A  M  U  Z  T  H  A  N  T  N  T  I  T  F
V  A  G  I  T  L  N  I  O  O  N  A  H  N  S
L  Z  F  N  L  A  N  E  I  Q  D  U  S  E  R
W  J  N  E  M  H  T  T  L  E  A  Q  N  R  E
H  D  B  X  Q  P  A  I  L  L  V  E  O  E  T
U  I  N  W  K  I  V  B  O  V  N  D  I  F  A
L  D  Y  T  L  W  A  F  Z  N  M  A  T  F  C
G  P  C  I  G  T  Y  P  N  I  G  F  A  I  O
T  O  F  G  I  E  P  Y  Q  V  I  F  L  D  L
Y  F  R  U  R  W  J  T  T  D  O  S  E  N  L
A  S  S  P  C  W  C  F  E  G  W  P  R  I  A
```

ADEQUATE   AFFILIATION   ALLOCATE

CONDOR   INDIFFERENT   LIBEL

PREFERENCE   PREY   RELATIONSHIP

REPUTATION   RESOURCES   SUITABLE

Let's Compose Sentences

Look back at the definitions and example sentences. Can you write a sentence for each of the words?

Adequate: _____

_____

Allocate: _____

_____

Indifferent: _____

_____

Libel: _____

_____

Affiliation: _____

_____

Condor: _____

_____

My Notes

Use this page for:
i. challenging spelling
ii. challenging definitions
iii. further practice

Lesson 2

Definitions

Authentic: real, original, not false.

Bystander: a spectator or onlooker who is not taking part in the situation or event.

Downright: absolutely or outright.

Customary: usual or traditional.

Exuberant: something or someone that is very energetic and unrestrained.

Flaw: a fault or a weakness in something or someone.

Example Sentences

The pizza from the Italian restaurant was so delicious because it was made with **authentic** ingredients.

As a **bystander**, I watched the parade pass by and felt proud to be a part of the community.

The new amusement park ride was **downright** thrilling! I can't wait to go back and ride it again.

It's **customary** for the birthday person to make a wish and blow out the candles on their cake.

The young dancer was **exuberant**, spinning and twirling with joy across the stage.

The beautiful painting had a small **flaw** in the corner, but it was still considered a masterpiece.

Let's Practice Spelling the Word

Keep Going!

au **th** authentic	au - then - tic →	→
by bystander	by - stand - er →	→
ow **igh** downright	down - right →	→
cus **om** customary	cus - tom - ar - y →	→
exu exuberant	ex - u - ber - ant →	→
aw flaw	flaw →	→

Now write each word in full.

authentic	→	→
bystanter	→	→
downright	→	→
customary	→	→
exuberant	→	→
flaw	→	→

	→	
	→	
	→	
	→	
	→	
	→	

	→	
	→	
	→	
	→	
	→	
	→	
	→	

Puzzle 2

```
T W I R L I N G X W U U B Y S
L T M N U U K G Z Z U J E P Y
I C S U O I C I L E D X I M R
Y N W X R Q E S U P U N X D A
A L G B I Y L V K B N R R E M
Z H I R W S U N E I K D A C O
T M C A E A D R N Y V C R E T
H W L S I D A G T A S I E I S
G F C C Y N I I O T J T D P U
I D V X T R N E E C H N N R C
R D P U X U O D N I Z E A E N
N D B B M X A E G T R H T T Q
W V T M A R L Q L H S T S S W
O P O L A M V Z D D G U Y A O
D C T P Y R T P E L D A B M Y
```

AUTHENTIC   BYSTANDER   COMMUNITY

CUSTOMARY   DELICIOUS   DOWNRIGHT

EXUBERANT   FLAW   INGREDIENTS

MASTERPIECE   PARADE   SPINNING

TWIRLING

Let's Compose Sentences

Look back at the definitions and example sentences. Can you write a sentence for each of the words?

Authentic: _____

_____

Bystander: _____

_____

Downright: _____

_____

Customary: _____

_____

Exuberant: _____

_____

Flaw: _____

_____

My Notes

Lesson 3

Definitions

Intimidate: to make someone feel scared or nervous, especially in order to get them to do what you want.

Mandatory: something required or necessary by law or rule.

Agitate: to make someone upset or worried, or to cause trouble or conflict.

Formidable: impressive or challenging, making someone feel like they need to be careful.

Liaison: a connection or relationship between two people or groups that helps them work together.

Punctual: being on time, arriving or doing something exactly when you are supposed to.

Example Sentences

The big, mean-looking dog was trying to **intimidate** the little puppy, but the puppy was brave and stood its ground.

In the UK, it is **mandatory** for all students to wear a uniform to school every day.

The long line at the amusement park was starting to **agitate** the children, who were getting restless and grumpy.

The steep mountain was **formidable**, and the hikers needed to be careful and take their time as they climbed up the trail.

The school principal acted as the **liaison** between the teachers and the parents, helping to keep everyone informed and working together.

It's important to be **punctual** and arrive at the movie theater on time, so you don't miss any of the movie.

Let's Practice Spelling the Word

ti ate intimidate	in - tim - i - date →	→
an da ory mandatory	man - da - to - ry →	→
gi ate agitate	ag - i - tate →	→
mid able formidable	for - mi - da - ble →	→
iai liaison	li - ai - son →	→
ct ua punctual	punc - tu - al →	→

Now write each word in full.

intimidate		→
mandatory		→
agitate		→
formidable		→
liaison		→
punctual		→

	$\longrightarrow$	
	$\longrightarrow$	
	$\longrightarrow$	
	$\longrightarrow$	
	$\longrightarrow$	
	$\longrightarrow$	

	$\longrightarrow$	
	$\longrightarrow$	
	$\longrightarrow$	
	$\longrightarrow$	
	$\longrightarrow$	
	$\longrightarrow$	

Puzzle 3

```
G  I  H  E  I  N  T  I  M  I  D  A  T  E  Y
E  G  M  E  E  O  N  T  I  M  E  Y  D  L  L
Z  W  W  P  B  B  O  D  K  T  W  R  E  H  A
T  P  W  P  R  X  D  N  H  N  M  A  R  T  U
H  C  A  C  M  E  K  M  H  V  O  S  L  A  T
B  A  O  G  U  M  S  I  O  E  Z  S  N  Z  C
W  F  Y  N  I  O  T  S  L  X  Y  E  T  G  N
S  K  S  L  N  T  Q  B  I  R  T  C  L  P  U
H  N  H  L  C  E  A  R  O  V  A  E  N  D  P
T  B  F  I  L  D  C  T  E  R  E  N  O  E  D
F  L  P  M  I  Y  A  T  E  Z  A  G  S  I  E
O  B  M  M  W  D  H  P  I  R  X  C  I  R  R
O  V  R  A  N  U  G  F  U  O  I  A  A  R  A
E  O  F  A  W  P  A  E  Y  V  N  T  I  O  C
F  I  M  N  W  R  A  W  A  P  V  L  L  W  S
```

AGITATE	CONNECTION	FORMIDABLE
IMPRESSIVE	INTIMIDATE	LIAISON
MANDATORY	NECESSARY	ON TIME
PUNCTUAL	SCARED	WORRIED

Let's Compose Sentences

Look back at the definitions and example sentences. Can you write a sentence for each of the words?

Intimidate: _____

_____

Mandatory: _____

_____

Agitate: _____

_____

Formidable: _____

_____

Liaison: _____

_____

Punctual: _____

_____

My Notes

Lesson 4

Definitions

Acknowledge: to recognize or admit that something is true or exists.

Loath: to be very unwilling to do something, or to dislike something very much.

Perturb: to make someone feel upset, worried, or anxious.

Tentative: not certain or definite, done in a careful and unsure way.

Bewilder: to confuse or puzzle someone, making them unsure of what is happening or what to do.

Mortify: to make someone feel ashamed or embarrassed, often in front of others.

Example Sentences

When the teacher called on him in class, Billy **acknowledged** that he didn't know the answer to the question.

Rebecca was **loath** to go to the party because she didn't like dancing in front of people.

The sudden loud noise outside the window **perturbed** the cat, causing it to jump up and run away.

Tim took a **tentative** step onto the high diving board, feeling a bit nervous about jumping into the pool.

The maze at the amusement park was so complicated that it **bewildered** the children, and they had to ask for help.

When Ava realized she had worn two different shoes to school, she was **mortified** and felt embarrassed.

ckn **ow** **dge** acknowledge	ac - knowl - edge →	→
oa **th** loath	loath →	→
er **ur** perturb	per - turb →	→
tat tentative	ten - ta - tive →	→
il bewilder	be - wil - der →	→
ti **fy** mortify	mor - ti - fy →	→

Now write each word in full.

acknowledge	→	→
loath	→	→
perturb	→	→
tentative	→	→
bewilder	→	→
mortify	→	→

	→	
	→	
	→	
	→	
	→	
	→	

	→	
	→	
	→	
	→	
	→	
	→	

Puzzle 4

```
A O O M B V D L M L O B B Z D
D D E Y O F F P E R T U R B R
S T M T Y R I X J A Y U P O E
G E C I E N T E L L H X B H D
J U W Y T N R I H U E I V Q L
D A R C R U T G F G K Q N O I
D Z L O S P O A D Y Y G M Q W
C W O N N M E E T B N R B D E
Q F U Z D D L H M I G V O E B
J W O U S W T Y L G V M S S V
E K I J O A I L T G E E J U T
P M H N O Z I E U Z O R H F E
U J K L F W X V E M R A B N S
W C N W N I R A B E H Y S O P
A J P U K I L V E X D V N C U
```

ACKNOWLEDGE   ADMIT   BEWILDER

CONFUSED   LOATH   MORTIFY

PERTURB   TENTATIVE   UNSURE

UNWILLING   UPSET

Let's Compose Sentences

Look back at the definitions and example sentences. Can you write a sentence for each of the words?

Acknowledge: _____

_____

Loath: _____

_____

Perturb: _____

_____

Tentative: _____

_____

Bewilder: _____

_____

Mortify: _____

_____

My Notes

Lesson 5

Definitions

Retort: to say something in response to a statement or question, especially in a quick and clever way.

Viewpoint: a way of thinking about or understanding something, based on personal opinions or experiences.

Canny: clever or shrewd, especially in a practical way.

Nimble: quick and light in movement, able to move easily and gracefully.

Substantial: large in size, amount, or degree, or having a solid and strong foundation.

Whim: a sudden and usually temporary desire or idea, often without much thought or planning.

Example Sentences

When the teacher asked if anyone had an answer to the question, Amelia **retorted**, "Yes, I do!"

Each person has their own **viewpoint** on what the best schooling for their child is, and it's important to respect everyone's opinions.

The **canny** detective was able to solve the mystery by using his clever thinking and attention to detail.

The **nimble** cat was able to climb up the tree and chase the bird, moving quickly and gracefully.

The **substantial** amount of money that was raised at the charity auction was enough to help many people in need.

It was just a **whim**, but Liam decided to try a new food for lunch and ended up loving it!

Let's Practice Spelling the Word

re / to / retort	re - tort	→
ie / oi / viewpoint	view - point	→
a / nn / canny	can - ny	→
m / ble / nimble	nim - ble	→
u / ti / substantial	sub - stan - tial	→
h / whim	whim	→

Now write each word in full.

retort	→	→
viewpoint	→	→
canny	→	→
nimble	→	→
substantial	→	→
whim	→	→

	→	
	→	
	→	
	→	
	→	
	→	

	→	
	→	
	→	
	→	
	→	
	→	

Puzzle 5

```
P O B H N H P O W X C Z L B I
Q Q Q H G I A P K P B P N D U
W U B L D R M Y W Q R N W W M
C L I J P L V B D H F P Z E K
I Y M C G O A K L T I L K R W
Y O Z D K B I R P E A M H H K
S R P P B R G F G I V T W S E
L L Z I J V J U T E N S V H D
D O R R N G J N S I S G V P N
E H S Q T I A L O K S C F T O
R Q W L V T O P J Q R Z Y R P
I R V P S E W N Y L G N U O S
S N V B C E D H P G N I E T E
E J U J I F D Y E A K G Q E R
D S B V X H Z Y C G B M S R M
```

CANNY	DESIRE	LARGE
NIMBLE	OPINION	QUICK
RESPOND	RETORT	SHREWD
SUBSTANTIAL	VIEWPOINT	WHIM

Let's Compose Sentences

Look back at the definitions and example sentences. Can you write a sentence for each of the words?

Retort:

_____

_____

Viewpoint:

_____

_____

Canny:

_____

_____

Nimble:

_____

_____

Substantial:

_____

_____

Whim:

_____

_____

My Notes

Lesson 6

Definitions

Abode: a place where someone lives or stays, such as a house or apartment.

Ascertain: to find out or discover something for certain, often by investigating or asking questions.

Elegant: neat, graceful, and attractive in a simple and refined way.

Precedent: an earlier event or action that is used as an example or rule to be followed in the future.

Agrarian: relating to farming or agriculture.

Delirious: confused, disoriented, and unable to think clearly, often due to illness or exhaustion.

Example Sentences

The old mansion was the perfect **abode** for the wealthy family, with its spacious rooms and beautiful gardens.

The investigative journalist was trying to **ascertain** the truth about what had happened, so he asked many questions.

The **elegant** ballerina danced gracefully across the stage, moving with fluid and effortless motions.

The court case set a **precedent** for how similar cases should be handled in the future.

The **agrarian** town was known for its fertile land and abundant crops, and many families made their living by farming.

When Emma came down with a high fever, she became **delirious**, muttering strange and confusing things.

a / de **abode**	a - bode →	
sc / ai **ascertain**	as - cer - tain →	
a **elegant**	el - e - gant →	
ece **precedent**	prec - e - dent →	
rar / ian **agrarian**	a - grar - i - an →	
ir **delirious**	del - ir - i - ous →	

Now write each word in full.

abode	→ →	
ascertain	→ →	
elegant	→ →	
precedent	→ →	
agrarian	→ →	
delirious	→ →	

	→	
	→	
	→	
	→	
	→	
	→	

	→	
	→	
	→	
	→	
	→	
	→	

Puzzle 6

```
X  W  A  G  X  P  R  E  C  E  D  E  N  T  N
A  S  X  G  Z  U  U  A  U  H  B  V  D  C  W
A  G  I  U  R  A  J  U  S  J  O  S  T  D  M
K  S  R  G  C  I  E  S  B  O  U  U  I  Q  Y
D  N  C  A  G  X  C  D  E  I  N  J  S  N  L
E  Q  F  E  R  R  N  U  D  G  V  R  C  E  T
T  S  E  R  R  I  A  F  L  B  G  Z  N  D  N
N  U  W  N  R  T  A  C  A  T  R  G  S  Y  A
E  O  B  L  E  C  A  N  E  S  U  U  J  Z  G
I  I  R  A  V  N  D  I  D  F  O  R  H  H  E
R  R  E  U  O  L  N  I  N  I  U  B  E  E  L
O  I  H  V  C  V  A  R  V  O  P  L  Z  D  E
S  L  P  G  S  U  S  E  R  Y  Z  K  C  O  Y
I  E  T  H  I  K  R  J  O  T  D  L  Z  B  U
D  D  F  D  D  P  R  L  V  U  S  E  M  A  K
```

ABODE   AGRARIAN   AGRICULTURE

ASCERTAIN   DELIRIOUS   DISCOVER

DISORIENTED   ELEGANT   GRACEFUL

HOUSE   PRECEDENT   PREVIOUS

Let's Compose Sentences

Look back at the definitions and example sentences. Can you write a sentence for each of the words?

Abode:

_____

_____

Ascertain:

_____

_____

Elegant:

_____

_____

Precedent:

_____

_____

Agrarian:

_____

_____

Delirious:

_____

_____

My Notes

Lesson 7

Definitions

Expatriate: a person who lives outside their home country, often for a long period of time.

Preclude: to prevent something from happening or make it impossible to happen.

Antiquated: old-fashioned and no longer used or relevant.

Demonstrative: showing or expressing strong feelings or opinions, often in a loud or dramatic way.

Intrepid: brave and willing to face danger or difficulty without fear.

Restorative: something that helps to bring back beauty, health, strength, or energy.

Example Sentences

The **expatriate** family lived in a foreign country for many years, making new friends and learning about different cultures.

The bad weather conditions **precluded** the team from playing the outdoor soccer game, forcing them to find an indoor alternative.

The antique car was considered **antiquated** by most people, as it was old-fashioned and didn't have modern features like air conditioning.

The **demonstrative** protestor held up a sign and shouted loudly, showing her strong feelings about the issue.

The **intrepid** adventurer climbed the tallest mountain, facing challenges and overcoming obstacles along the way.

The **restorative** yoga class was a great way for the tired and stressed students to relax and recharge their bodies and minds.

Let's Practice Spelling the Word

Practice the Tricky letters		
expatriate — pat / ria	ex - pa - tri - ate → →	
preclude — ude	pre - clude → →	
antiquated — qua	an - ti - quat - ed →	
demonstrative — stra	de - mon - stra - tive →	
intrepid — tre / id	in - trep - id →	
restorative — re / at	re - stor - a - tive → →	

Now write each word in full.

expatriate		→ →
preclude		→ →
antiquated		→ →
demonstrative		→ →
intrepid		→ →
restorative		→ →

	→	
	→	
	→	
	→	
	→	
	→	

	→	
	→	
	→	
	→	
	→	
	→	

Puzzle 7

```
L Y B M F A I O U T S I D E B
O T S R N P R E V E N T P Y G
V L L A T B C R W B Y E P V
Q B D Z V V H O E E V X J I
X B S F P S E Q T E I T E D N
U I Q R A G W A P T W P V E M
V P T L S S I Q A C E F I T M
N J R P O R H R F E S Z T A E
O E S E T T I Q H R J A U G
Q M J A C S D B O C R F R Q R
A R P N N L F J N N H A O I A
M X D O M B U T W S E N T T H
E U M I R P T D S B E D S N C
F E E L I N G S E K L E E A E
D O F I N T R E P I D P R F R
```

ANTIQUATED	BRAVE	DEMONSTRATIVE
EXPATRIATE	FEELINGS	INTREPID
OLD-FASHIONED	OUTSIDE	PRECLUDE
PREVENT	RECHARGE	RESTORATIVE

Let's Compose Sentences

Look back at the definitions and example sentences. Can you write a sentence for each of the words?

Expatriate:

_____

_____

Preclude:

_____

_____

Antiquated:

_____

_____

Demonstrative:

_____

_____

Intrepid:

_____

_____

Restorative:

_____

_____

My Notes

Lesson 8

Definitions

Addict: a person who has a strong desire or need for something and can't easily stop using it.

Competent: capable of doing something well or effectively, with the necessary skills and knowledge.

Contrast: the difference between two things, often shown by comparing them.

Devious: behaving in a sneaky or untrustworthy way, often to get what one wants.

Antagonize: to cause anger or hostility towards someone, often by doing or saying something that is provocative or offensive.

Component: a part or piece of something, especially one of several parts that make up a whole.

Example Sentences

Charlotte was a chocolate **addict**. She couldn't resist eating the whole bar even if it made her feel sick afterwards.

The **competent** teacher was able to explain the complex math problem in a way that all the students could understand.

The **contrast** between the hot and humid weather and the cool and comfortable air-conditioned room was striking.

The **devious** cat would often wait until its owner was sleeping, and then sneak into the kitchen to steal food from the counter.

The teasing comments made by the classmates **antagonized** the sensitive student, causing her to feel upset and frustrated.

The **component** parts of the car engine were carefully assembled by the mechanic, who made sure everything was in its proper place.

dd **ict** addict	ad - dict ⟶	⟶
ent competent	com - pe - tent ⟶	⟶
ast contrast	con - trast ⟶	⟶
i **ous** devious	de - vi - ous ⟶	⟶
an **tag** antagonize	an - tag - o - nize ⟶	⟶
ent component	com - po - nent ⟶	⟶

Now write each word in full.

addict	⟶	⟶
competent	⟶	⟶
contrast	⟶	⟶
devious	⟶	⟶
antagonize	⟶	⟶
component	⟶	⟶

	→	
	→	
	→	
	→	
	→	
	→	

	→	
	→	
	→	
	→	
	→	
	→	

Puzzle 8

```
D K H H O S T I L E G A Z N X
P E T T D U W X F Y U M S U P
H A V Y Y B M W E S X C Y Z T
V Y N I U H V H Y R A Q H B C
J P Z T O O R I B J U M T G I
A H N S A U E N X K Q R R Q D
T T B U J G S R G C X P O T D
L N V N I A O T A P F P W N A
J E L Y V K S N E C D L T E L
M N U B S A X R I E S L S T A
V O Y E R C A J L Z B O U E R
I P Q T U P E L L J E Q R P E
I M N X M A I K I I H R T M V
E O P O A K N X E P H K N O E
C C C D S U W W K V Y S U C S
```

ADDICT   ANTAGONIZE   COMPARE

COMPETENT   COMPONENT   CONTRAST

DEVIOUS   HOSTILE   SEVERAL

SKILLED   UNTRUSTWORTHY

Let's Compose Sentences

Look back at the definitions and example sentences. Can you write a sentence for each of the words?

Addict: _____

_____

Competent: _____

_____

Contrast: _____

_____

Devious: _____

_____

Antagonize: _____

_____

Component: _____

_____

My Notes

Lesson 9

Definitions

Demeanor: the way a person behaves or acts, especially in public or in front of others.

Emphasize: to give special importance or attention to something, often by speaking or writing about it in a strong way.

Bamboozle: to deceive or trick someone, often by making them believe something that is not true.

Consult: to seek advice or information from someone who has more knowledge or experience in a particular area.

Devastate: to cause serious damage or harm, often destroying or ruining something completely.

Irrelevant: not related or important to a particular situation or discussion, and not having any effect on the outcome.

Example Sentences

The young musician had a calm and confident **demeanor**, which impressed everyone who met him.

The teacher **emphasized** the importance of studying hard for the test, telling the students that their grades would determine their future success.

The clever magician **bamboozled** the audience with his illusions, making them believe he could levitate and disappear into thin air.

The worried parents **consulted** the doctor about their child's health, asking for advice and information on how to help him get better.

The **devastating** hurricane caused widespread damage, destroying many homes and leaving thousands of people homeless.

The discussion about the latest movie was **irrelevant** to the meeting, as it had nothing to do with the agenda or the purpose of the gathering.

Let's Practice Spelling the Word

de **ean** demeanor	de - mean - or →	→
em **ph** emphasize	em - pha - size →	
oo bamboozle	bam - boo - zle	
u consult	con - sult →	
as devastate	dev - as - tate →	
rr **ev** **ant** irrelevant	ir - rel - e - vant →	

Now write each word in full.

demeanor		→
emphasize		→
bamboozle		→
consult		→
devastate		→
irrelevant		→

Puzzle 9

```
U Y W H H V H L A I B J E O G
D N J D E M P H A S I Z E M D
B E I B A M B O O Z L E W C K
O E V M X Q L B V C B T B V I
M Q H A P S O D W I T Q N U F
T G B A S O S G K D E T H E O
N T O F V T R K U P H J D C I
A W Q Z I I A T W J M Z A N O
V T D D E I O T A K Z F H A W
E L F L G Y J R E N I V E T T
L U F A A S V L B I T R C R K
E S N K M W I G Y S P B I O C
R N C Q A X V Y I Q Z O V P I
R O N V D R W C P Z Q L D M R
I C D E M E A N O R D R A I T
```

ADVICE   BAMBOOZLE   BEHAVIOR

CONSULT   DAMAGE   DEMEANOR

DEVASTATE   EMPHASIZE   IMPORTANCE

IRRELEVANT   TRICK   UNIMPORTANT

Let's Compose Sentences

Look back at the definitions and example sentences. Can you write a sentence for each of the words?

Demeanor: _____

_____

Emphasize: _____

_____

Bamboozle: _____

_____

Consult: _____

_____

Devastate: _____

_____

Irrelevant: _____

_____

My Notes

Lesson 10

Definitions

Guarantee: a promise or assurance that something will happen or be true. It can be given verbally or in writing.

Hybrid: a mixture of two or more different things, often resulting in a new and unique combination.

Irate: angry or upset, to the point of being furious.

Lurk: to hide or stay concealed, often in order to watch or spy on someone without being seen.

Murky: dark and unclear, often because of a lack of light or because something is blocking the view.

Nurture: to care for and support something or someone, helping them to grow and develop.

Example Sentences

The toy store offered a **guarantee** that the new action figure would be delivered in time for the birthday party, or the customer would receive a full refund.

The **hybrid** car is a mixture of electric and gasoline power, providing a more efficient and environmentally friendly way to drive.

The **irate** driver honked his horn and shouted at the other driver who cut him off in traffic, causing a dangerous road rage incident.

The curious cat liked to **lurk** behind the curtains and watch the birds outside, waiting for the perfect moment to pounce.

The **murky** water in the pond was so dark that it was difficult to see the fish swimming below the surface.

The loving parents **nurtured** their children, providing them with food, shelter, and education, and helping them to grow into happy and successful adults.

Let's Practice Spelling the Word

ua **ee** guarantee	guar - an - tee ⟶	⟶
y **i** hybrid	hy - brid ⟶	⟶
ir irate	i - rate	
u lurk	lurk ⟶	
u murky	murk - y ⟶	⟶
nu **tu** nurture	nur - ture ⟶	⟶

Now write each word in full.

guarantee	⟶	⟶
hybrid	⟶	
irate	⟶	⟶
lurk	⟶	⟶
murky	⟶	⟶
nurture	⟶	

	→	
	→	
	→	
	→	
	→	
	→	

	→	
	→	
	→	
	→	
	→	
	→	

Puzzle 10

```
I M K Y C W L N U R T U R E P
R R E R E A O N D E T P K E I
U O A V K A R E V V E I T B Q
V D D T E O L E J Y L D V Y R
D F Z P E A G Y V L Y N E Z L
T F V S E A V A M K B L F Z W
E S P C G L N J S E Z U K L C
H E N R J X O J E T C U Z S Q
F O Z Y O X R T P R T O K D E
C Q J W X M N T L A D N X T R
U A V W Y A I D Z E I K Y G U
G D M K R N K S W L R U R C T
K A R A G M R F E C B Z G L X
F U U F E D U Y N N Y Y N M I
M G X V D R L C S U H U A R M
```

ANGRY	CARE	CONCEALED
GUARANTEE	HYBRID	IRATE
LURK	MIXTURE	MURKY
NURTURE	PROMISE	UNCLEAR

Let's Compose Sentences

Look back at the definitions and example sentences. Can you write a sentence for each of the words?

Guarantee: _____

_____

Hybrid: _____

_____

Irate: _____

_____

Lurk: _____

_____

Murky: _____

_____

Nurture: _____

_____

My Notes

Lesson 11

Definitions

Abdicate: to give up or renounce a position of power or responsibility, such as that of a king or queen.

Docile: easy to control or manage, often because of a willingness to comply or follow orders.

Grueling: extremely difficult or tiring and requiring a lot of effort or endurance.

Ludicrous: silly or absurd to the point of being ridiculous.

Brawl: a noisy and violent argument or fight, usually involving many people.

Erode: to wear away or damage gradually, often because of natural processes such as wind, water, or ice.

Example Sentences

The king **abdicated** his throne, giving up his power and responsibilities to his son, who would become the new king.

The **docile** dog followed its owner's commands, sitting, staying, and rolling over whenever asked.

The **grueling** hike up the mountain was difficult and tiring, but the stunning view from the top was well worth the effort.

The clown's antics were so **ludicrous** that the children couldn't stop laughing.

The **brawl** at the school cafeteria started when two students had a disagreement over who was next in line.

The river **eroded** the banks over time, creating deep canyons and forming new land masses in the process.

Let's Practice Spelling the Word

bd — abdicate	ab - di - cate →	→
ci le — docile	doc - ile →	→
ue — grueling	gru - el - ing →	→
ous — ludicrous	lu - di - crous →	→
aw — brawl	brawl →	→
er ode — erode	e - rode →	→

Now write each word in full.

abdicate	→	→
docile	→	→
grueling	→	→
ludicrous	→	→
brawl	→	→
erode	→	→

Practice
makes
Perfect!

	→	
	→	
	→	
	→	
	→	
	→	

	→	
	→	
	→	
	→	
	→	
	→	

Puzzle 11

```
R W W A R E V Q A E V P B S I
U E R I B T T I Z B A Y B D L
S X N C P D R F O Q S S L S E
U J P O L O I D M L R U Y V B
O U O D U F D C L B E R R L C
R B B C O N L P A L J N V D J
C S U S B I C Y S T U Q C R T
I Y A C N C E E D G E Y Y E L
D C E Y U W I Q N M A V W K U
U D O C I L E I Y W Z U Y P C
L Q S K T G L B A M H D E M I
J Q O E J E W R Q V O G D J F
X H R H U V A Y D P E C O S F
O T U R Y E R K Y M V R R B I
C D G E W A B V A H E C E Y D
```

ABDICATE   ABSURD   BRAWL

DIFFICULT   DOCILE   EASY

ERODE   GRUELING   LUDICROUS

RENOUNCE   VIOLENCE   WEAR AWAY

Let's Compose Sentences

Look back at the definitions and example sentences. Can you write a sentence for each of the words?

Abdicate:

_____

_____

Docile:

_____

_____

Grueling:

_____

_____

Ludicrous:

_____

_____

Brawl:

_____

_____

Erode:

_____

_____

My Notes

Lesson 12

Definitions

Hurtle: to move or be thrown with great force in a dangerous or uncontrolled manner.

Murder: the illegal and intentional killing of one person by another.

Counterfeit: an imitation or fake of something, made with the intent to deceive or defraud.

Flagrant: obvious and intentional in a way that is wrong or violates rules or laws.

Inundate: to overwhelm or flood with a large amount of something, often water or information.

Notorious: well-known or famous for something bad or negative.

Example Sentences

The car spun out of control and **hurtled** off the road, crashing into a ditch.

The police arrested the suspect for **murder**, after they found large traces of blood in his house.

The store owner realized that the money he had received was **counterfeit**, after he tried to use it at a different store and was told it was fake.

The **flagrant** violation of the school rules, such as cheating on a test, would result in serious consequences.

The heavy rain caused the river to overflow its banks, **inundating** the surrounding neighborhoods.

He was a **notorious** criminal because everybody knew of his daring escapes from prison and his ability to elude the police.

Let's Practice Spelling the Word

ur hurtle	hur - tle →	→
ur murder	mur - der →	→
ei counterfeit	coun - ter - feit →	→
ra flagrant	fla - grant →	→
un inundate	in - un - date →	→
ri **ous** notorious	no - to - ri - ous →	→

Now write each word in full.

hurtle	→	→
murder	→	→
counterfeit	→	→
flagrant	→	→
inundate	→	→
notorious	→	→

Puzzle 12

```
K  F  L  A  G  R  A  N  T  F  V  Q  F  C  R
F  I  X  N  V  Y  I  W  N  V  Z  V  U  Q  P
R  A  L  L  P  D  K  N  R  V  J  A  T  S  N
R  T  M  L  U  J  F  Z  U  O  L  A  U  H  W
N  U  Q  O  B  Z  Q  K  R  N  N  V  G  T  T
D  Z  C  C  U  B  D  Y  F  K  D  G  S  G  I
N  X  M  O  T  S  T  B  Q  W  S  A  T  M  E
T  J  W  X  V  S  W  H  S  U  B  G  T  L  F
B  U  T  C  J  B  T  B  O  V  L  S  U  E  R
A  E  N  L  F  K  F  I  I  R  E  O  F  H  E
J  F  T  K  O  E  R  E  E  R  Z  F  W  W  T
E  D  L  K  U  O  V  D  N  S  F  E  O  R  N
S  C  P  M  T  I  R  D  M  P  I  K  R  E  U
O  W  V  O  H  U  R  T  L  E  D  A  H  V  O
D  U  N  T  M  I  D  E  C  R  W  F  T  O  C
```

COUNTERFEIT   FAKE   FAMOUS

FLAGRANT   HURTLE   INUNDATE

KILL   MURDER   NOTORIOUS

OVERWHELM   THROW   WRONG

Let's Compose Sentences

Look back at the definitions and example sentences. Can you write a sentence for each of the words?

Hurtle:

_____

_____

Murder:

_____

_____

Counterfeit:

_____

_____

Flagrant:

_____

_____

Inundate:

_____

_____

Notorious:

_____

_____

My Notes

Lesson 13

Definitions

Acquire: to gain possession of something.

Correspond: to be in communication with someone, through letters, email, or other forms of communication.

Deceitful: trickery or dishonest behavior with the intent to fool someone.

Exposition: a comprehensive explanation or presentation of information or ideas, with the goal of educating or informing others.

Alternative: an option or choice that differs from the usual or expected.

Consecutive: following one after another, in a continuous or uninterrupted sequence.

Example Sentences

Sam **acquired** a new bike by saving her allowance for several months.

He **corresponded** with his pen pal every week by sending letters.

The **deceitful** salesperson tried to convince the customer to buy a faulty product.

The science **exposition** showcased exciting experiments and projects from local students.

Instead of driving, they decided to bike as an **alternative**.

The basketball team won three **consecutive** games, breaking their losing streak.

Let's Practice Spelling the Word

cq **ui** acquire	ac - quired →	→
rr correspond	cor - re - spond →	→
c **ei** deceitful	de - ceit - ful →	→
x exposition	ex - po - si - tion →	→
al **na** alternative	al - ter - na - tive →	→
ec **u** consecutive	con - sec - u - tive →	→

Now write each word in full.

acquire	→	→
correspond	→	→
deceitful	→	→
exposition	→	→
alternative	→	→
consecutive	→	→

	→	
	→	
	→	
	→	
	→	
	→	

	→	
	→	
	→	
	→	
	→	
	→	

Puzzle 13

```
S D V A A C Q U I R E E G I G
M E P R E S E N T A T I O N Q
E R Q V Z U E V D G T Z E M N
G X B U S Y M B Q Y V N V K O
I E P J E D P W G W M U I E I
R V G O P N O U E M D L T K T
Y I H X S G C H W N U A A T P
K T R I H I K E O F C N N S O
Q U S B H J T P T I S P R E J
T C T T J C S I N U S W E N W
K E C X E E E U O Q E K T O Q
L S G Q R C M U G N S Y L H M
P N G R E M A L C T S Q A S A
U O O D O E J I W W O W Q I R
J C W C L A K Q A F P C M D Z
```

ACQUIRE   ALTERNATIVE   COMMUNICATE

CONSECUTIVE   CORRESPOND   DECEITFUL

DISHONEST   EXPOSITION   OPTION

POSSESS   PRESENTATION   SEQUENCE

Let's Compose Sentences

Look back at the definitions and example sentences. Can you write a sentence for each of the words?

Acquire: _____

_____

Correspond: _____

_____

Deceitful: _____

_____

Exposition: _____

_____

Alternative: _____

_____

Consecutive: _____

_____

My Notes

Lesson 14

Definitions

Diversity: different types of people, ideas, or things, making up a varied community or environment.

Famished: extremely hungry.

Boycott: to refuse to participate in or support something as a form of protest or demonstration.

Dawdle: to waste time or move slowly, often without a sense of purpose.

Estimate: a rough calculation or prediction of a quantity or value.

Attribute: a quality, characteristic, or feature that is associated with someone or something.

Example Sentences

The school celebrated **diversity** by hosting a cultural fair where students showcased their heritage and traditions.

After playing outside all day, the kids were **famished** and couldn't wait to eat dinner.

Some customers chose to **boycott** the store because of their unethical business practices.

The students were **dawdling** in the hallway even though the class had already started.

The contractor had given an **estimate** of the cost to repair the roof, but the final bill was higher because of unexpected expenses.

Kindness and generosity are **attributes** that make a person truly great.

di **si** diversity	di - ver - si - ty →	→
fa famished	fam - ished →	→
tt boycott	boy - cott →	→
aw dawdle	daw - dle →	→
ti **ate** estimate	es - ti - mate →	→
att **ute** attribute	at - trib - ute →	→

Now write each word in full.

diversity		→
famished		→
boycott		→
dawdle		→
estimate		→
attribute		→

Practice makes Perfect!

Puzzle 14

```
C H A R A C T E R I S T I C A
F Y C S D H H U N G R Y P T P
Y W A S T E T I M E G T T R U
Q E L I K W P R R J O R O V X
Z R C X H R W D U B I T Y N N
F T U U S I U W B B E L B U M
A A L F L W Y J U S T V T X V
M M A K Y P Z T T N K Y G S I
I W T Y B O E H I T A E P H N
S E I P T W K B C S O S W U V
H L O X N E R U B P R C D E R
E D N W H N I C V Y F E Y A R
D W C D M P B R I Z M X V O W
O A O E S T I M A T E L H I B
N D D A O R O K Q V G N I J D
```

ATTRIBUTE	BOYCOTT	CALCULATION
CHARACTERISTIC	DAWDLE	DIVERSITY
ESTIMATE	FAMISHED	HUNGRY
PROTEST	VARIETY	WASTE TIME

Let's Compose Sentences

Look back at the definitions and example sentences. Can you write a sentence for each of the words?

Diversity: _____

_____

Famished: _____

_____

Boycott: _____

_____

Dawdle: _____

_____

Estimate: _____

_____

Attribute: _____

_____

My Notes

Lesson 15

Definitions

Despondent: feeling very sad, hopeless, and discouraged.

Flabbergasted: completely shocked and surprised, often in a positive way.

Implore: to ask or beg for something very strongly and with great urgency.

Magnitude: the size or scale of something, often in terms of importance or impact.

Dishearten: to make someone feel discouraged or lose hope.

Hilarious: extremely funny and causing a lot of laughter.

Example Sentences

After losing the championship game, the team was **despondent** and didn't feel like talking to anyone.

When Aaron found a hundred-dollar bill lying on the sidewalk, he was completely **flabbergasted**.

Faye **implored** her sister not to tell their mother that she had drunk the wine.

The **magnitude** of the earthquake was so strong that it caused buildings to crumble and roads to crack.

The bad news about the canceled trip **disheartened** the kids, who were looking forward to it for months.

The clown's silly jokes were **hilarious**, and everyone was laughing so hard their stomachs hurt.

Let's Practice Spelling the Word

es / ent despondent	de - spond - ent →	→
abb / ast flabbergasted	flab - ber - gast - ed →	→
ore implore	im - plore →	→
gn / ude magnitude	mag - ni - tude →	→
ear dishearten	dis - heart - en →	→
ar / ious hilarious	hi - lar - i - ous →	→

Now write each word in full.

despondent		→ →
flabbergasted		→ →
implore		→ →
magnitude		→ →
dishearten		→ →
hilarious		→ →

	→	
	→	
	→	
	→	
	→	
	→	

	→	
	→	
	→	
	→	
	→	
	→	

Puzzle 15

```
T D E S P O N D E N T Y H K S
D I S C O U R A G E F I T C C
D Q A X S M D E H U P E A G Y
E D X Y T H F G N X P L Q O S
T S I V F L A N X D E W X K A
S E U I Q N Y O G U O L I K B
A N E R R S E Q E S R M U M E
G L A D P M J T U R O M J T G
R L T P U R S O R F O G O H W
E O Q Y K T I K T A O L U R H
B M D M M R I S X A E N P Z F
B J V S A Y W N E N R H H M S
A I M L V D Y D G D P D S D I
L Q I X M J F N C A Z Y O I E
F H O P E L E S S B M K D Z D
```

BEG

DESPONDENT

DISCOURAGE

DISHEARTEN

FLABBERGASTED

FUNNY

HILARIOUS

HOPELESS

IMPLORE

MAGNITUDE

SCALE

SURPRISED

Let's Compose Sentences

Look back at the definitions and example sentences. Can you write a sentence for each of the words?

Despondent: _____

_____

Flabbergasted: _____

_____

Implore: _____

_____

Magnitude: _____

_____

Dishearten: _____

_____

Hilarious: _____

_____

My Notes

Lesson 16

Definitions

Incredulous: not able to believe something or someone because it seems too strange or unbelievable.

Prior: happening or existing before something else.

Industrious: hardworking and always busy, with a lot of energy and determination.

Ensue: to happen as a result of something else, often in a natural or expected way.

Impartial: treating everyone equally, without favoring one person or group over another.

Recede: to move further away.

Example Sentences

The young girl was **incredulous** when she found out she had won first prize in the science fair.

It's important to have a proper warm-up **prior** to playing any sport to avoid injury.

The ants are always so **industrious**, working hard to gather food and build their nests.

After the storm passed, a beautiful rainbow **ensued**.

The judge must always be **impartial** and make decisions based on the facts, not personal feelings.

When the tide goes out, the water **recedes** and reveals the sandy beach.

Let's Practice Spelling the Word

ul **ous** incredulous	in - cred - u - lous →	
io prior	pri - or →	
ri **ous** industrious	in - dus - tri - ous →	
en **ue** ensue	en - sue →	
tia impartial	im - par - tial →	
cede recede	re - cede →	

Now write each word in full.

incredulous	→ →	
prior	→ →	
industrious	→ →	
ensue	→ →	
impartial	→ →	
recede	→ →	

Practice
makes
Perfect!

	→	
	→	
	→	
	→	
	→	
	→	

	→	
	→	
	→	
	→	
	→	
	→	

Puzzle 16

```
P R I O R Q P J Q K Y F R W R
W F M Z D D D H F S A Q Y E P
J W P G J P X G Q I J C C H I
W C A E S U H A R I M E V N X
Z L R G X U D U G O D C D Q K
S G T Y N A O T Y E G U D D Q
G Y I L T I B L E N S W E U I
F A A H G F K D U T C Z M H I
N O L Y D L N R R D O W G S M
V J L M F W Y I O V E E R V B
E M M L T V O D A W R R R W Y
U E S I O U C G J O D L C T L
S D V F S W V U F F Z R B N F
N A H L U E W E V M S R A Z I
E F O E I P B Y Z T V F Y H Q
```

BEFORE	ENSUE	FADE
FAIR	FOLLOW	HARDWORKING
IMPARTIAL	INCREDULOUS	INDUSTRIOUS
PRIOR	RECEDE	

Let's Compose Sentences

Look back at the definitions and example sentences. Can you write a sentence for each of the words?

Incredulous: _____

_____

Prior: _____

_____

Industrious: _____

_____

Ensue: _____

_____

Impartial: _____

_____

Recede: _____

_____

My Notes

Lesson 17

Definitions

Figment: something that is imagined or made up in the mind and is not real.

Momentum: the force or energy that keeps an object moving forward.

Rant: to talk in a loud, angry way about something for a long time.

Tamper: to interfere with or change something, often in a way that is not allowed.

Initiate: to start or begin something.

Negligent: not taking proper care or attention to something, often resulting in harm or mistakes.

Example Sentences

The unicorn that the little girl claimed to have seen, was just a **figment** of her imagination and not a real animal.

The roller coaster picked up **momentum** as it went down the steep hill.

The angry customer **ranted** about the poor service at the restaurant.

Tampering with the evidence in a crime investigation is a serious offense and can lead to serious consequences.

The leader of the group **initiated** the discussion on how to raise money for the charity event.

The driver was found to be **negligent** for not stopping at the red light.

ent figment	fig - ment	→
um momentum	mo - men - tum	→
an rant	rant	→
am tamper	tam - per	→
iti initiate	in - i - ti - ate	→
gli negligent	neg - li - gent	→

Now write each word in full.

figment		→
momentum		→
rant		→
tamper		→
initiate		→
negligent		→

	→	
	→	
	→	
	→	
	→	
	→	

	→	
	→	
	→	
	→	
	→	
	→	

Puzzle 17

```
I N T E R F E R E F N I G E B
R Z U T D L L E F I S N Q B J
D A A D X M R Z X G O B I L A
D J N R X Z W B G M H W F N L
J C F T I M K B O E N P G E M
K O N E G L I G E N T R H O U
L F T R S L S W T Y H M J B
U S D D C T E M S Y Z E J O L
K S Z E I A G T F E N L D S O
R C Y Z N I T X A T L O L X I
E K G S V I C S U I W E A Z F
P C R W A X G M U U T K R Q N
M S E L Y X N A X J F I Y A D
A F N T X X I Z M E Z Y N S C
T P E S K J J G M I J R F I G
```

ANGRY   BEGIN   CARELESS

ENERGY   FIGMENT   IMAGINED

INITIATE   INTERFERE   MOMENTUM

NEGLIGENT   RANT   TAMPER

Let's Compose Sentences

Look back at the definitions and example sentences. Can you write a sentence for each of the words?

Figment:

_____

_____

Momentum:

_____

_____

Rant:

_____

_____

Tamper:

_____

_____

Initiate:

_____

_____

Negligent:

_____

_____

Lesson 18

Definitions

Signify: to show, indicate or mean something.

Vengeance: seeking revenge or punishment for a wrong that has been committed.

Void: an empty space or a lack of something.

Lethal: deadly or capable of causing death.

Persist: to continue doing something despite difficulties or opposition.

Status: the relative importance, rank, or position of someone or something.

Example Sentences

The red light **signifies** that it's time to stop.

The employees banded together to seek **vengeance** against the CEO for their unfair treatment.

The room felt empty and **void** of life.

The poison was **lethal** and could kill within minutes.

Despite the setbacks she had experienced in France, she **persisted** in her efforts to learn French.

She was proud of her high **status** as the class president.

gn fy **signify**	sig - ni - fy →	→
ean **vengeance**	venge - ance →	→
oi **void**	void →	→
th al **lethal**	le - thal →	→
si **persist**	per - sist →	→
us **status**	sta - tus →	→

Now write each word in full.

signify	→	→
vengeance	→	→
void	→	→
lethal	→	→
persist	→	→
status	→	→

	→	
	→	
	→	
	→	
	→	
	→	

	→	
	→	
	→	
	→	
	→	
	→	

Puzzle 18

```
L E T H A L R K T L G P X Z D
D R A R R J Y V A J X O V J V
E L D X A J B O Y D B N J E R
Z V C D L T W I Z A Y S N A S
B C A S N M J D D P K G N I C
C F M S P N T B G A E K G Q F
Q A E E V H F C S A P N J E K
I M A U R K I U N M I V R A T
V Q N T O R O C T F S I L I S
F Q I J R N E S Y B R J L R I
F X N C O B H H U I Y N E L S
Y E G S Y W A D W T G T R B R
Y Q I I Z Y L O V C A B P V E
P O V C O N T I N U E T M M P
P R E V E N G E D P D S S O E
```

CONTINUE	EMPTY	LETHAL
MEANING	PERSIST	POISONOUS
RANK	REVENGE	SIGNIFY
STATUS	VENGEANCE	VOID

Let's Compose Sentences

Look back at the definitions and example sentences. Can you write a sentence for each of the words?

Signify:

_____

_____

Vengeance:

_____

_____

Void:

_____

_____

Lethal:

_____

_____

Persist:

_____

_____

Status:

_____

_____

My Notes

Lesson 19

Definitions

Acrid: having a strong and unpleasant taste or smell.

Bleak: very unhappy or without hope.

Gruesome: horrible and shocking, often involving violence or death.

Intensified: something which is made stronger or more intense.

Unscathed: not hurt, damaged or affected by something.

Candid: honest and straightforward, not trying to hide anything.

Example Sentences

The smell of the spoiled milk was so **acrid** that it made everyone in the room gag.

The sky was gray and the wind was strong, making the scenery outside look gloomy and **bleak**.

The horror movie they watched had many **gruesome** scenes that made them all cover their eyes.

The heat of the day **intensified** as the sun rose higher in the sky.

Despite falling from his bike, he was **unscathed** and able to get back up and continue riding.

In the job interview, she answered all the questions with a **candid** and straightforward approach.

Let's Practice Spelling the Word

Keep Going!

ac **i** acrid	ac - rid ⟶	⟶
ea **k** bleak	bleak ⟶	⟶
ue gruesome	grue - some ⟶	⟶
si **fie** intensified	in - ten - si - fied ⟶	⟶
th unscathed	un - scathed ⟶	⟶
a candid	can - did ⟶	⟶

Now write each word in full.

acrid		⟶ ⟶
bleak		⟶ ⟶
gruesome		⟶ ⟶
intensified		⟶ ⟶
unscathed		⟶ ⟶
candid		⟶ ⟶

Practice
makes
Perfect!

	→	
	→	
	→	
	→	
	→	
	→	

	→	
	→	
	→	
	→	
	→	
	→	

Puzzle 19

```
S  G  R  C  B  U  S  A  O  L  K  A  E  L  B
T  X  R  O  R  E  B  A  M  U  E  P  M  P  U
R  U  B  U  F  R  M  Y  D  N  X  L  J  N  S
O  Z  C  F  E  S  R  T  W  L  K  G  H  V  W
N  W  S  Q  D  S  X  E  Y  Y  L  A  L  X  A
G  F  R  M  D  E  O  Q  E  F  R  A  Y  Q  C
C  T  F  D  D  W  I  M  P  M  E  U  M  W  R
F  A  X  A  V  E  L  F  E  G  B  I  O  P  I
Z  I  N  J  V  D  H  D  I  Q  D  G  O  H  D
P  K  J  D  J  N  A  T  I  S  T  U  L  H  T
B  L  Y  N  I  A  S  A  A  S  N  U  G  K  B
R  H  R  Q  P  D  G  V  E  C  W  E  C  O  B
A  Y  A  V  D  Z  O  N  O  A  S  I  T  B  L
T  Q  C  S  P  B  O  L  L  J  S  N  M  N  N
R  X  S  Y  D  H  A  V  V  Y  L  E  U  N  I
```

ACRID   BLEAK   CANDID

GLOOMY   GRUESOME   HONEST

INTENSIFIED   SCARY   STRONG

UNHARMED   UNSCATHED

Let's Compose Sentences

Look back at the definitions and example sentences. Can you write a sentence for each of the words?

Acrid:

_____

_____

Bleak:

_____

_____

Gruesome:

_____

_____

Intensified:

_____

_____

Unscathed:

_____

_____

Candid:

_____

_____

My Notes

Lesson 20

Definitions

Haggle: to argue or bargain over the price of something.

Ponder: to think carefully and deeply about something.

Annihilate: to completely destroy or eliminate something.

Catastrophe: a very bad event or disaster.

Impede: to slow down or block the progress of something or someone.

Robust: strong and healthy, or able to withstand a lot of stress or pressure.

Example Sentences

Grandma and the street vendor **haggled** over the price of the new hat.

Jeremy said that he needed some time to **ponder** over his options, before making a decision.

The virus **annihilated** the entire elderly population of the town.

The earthquake was a real **catastrophe** and left many people homeless.

The roadwork ahead is going to **impede** our progress and cause a delay.

The company's financial position was **robust**, with strong earnings and growth.

Let's Practice Spelling the Word

gg **i** haggle	haggle →	→
er ponder	pon - der →	→
nn **ihi** annihilate	an - ni - hi - late →	→
ro **phe** catastrophe	ca - tas - tro - phe →	→
ede impede	impede →	→
bu robust	ro - bust →	→

Now write each word in full.

haggle		→ →
ponder		→ →
annihilate		→ →
catastrophe		→ →
impede		→ →
robust		→ →

	→	
	→	
	→	
	→	
	→	
	→	

	→	
	→	
	→	
	→	
	→	
	→	

Puzzle 20

```
J  V  T  E  I  F  R  E  T  S  A  S  I  D  Q
C  S  A  B  L  O  C  K  D  P  F  J  C  U  W
S  O  L  N  E  O  M  D  N  U  J  T  A  T  M
G  D  N  G  N  F  Z  F  M  I  B  R  T  B  F
H  X  U  S  E  I  D  J  X  E  R  A  H  W  S
Q  M  Y  R  I  H  H  X  R  E  V  Z  S  Z  A
V  H  I  P  A  D  P  I  L  C  B  I  Q  W  C
Z  A  M  O  F  B  E  O  L  T  M  P  I  I  J
S  X  Y  B  H  I  L  R  R  A  S  Z  D  Z  X
E  E  O  D  P  M  D  E  R  T  T  U  N  I  E
T  L  R  Y  Q  Y  Q  D  W  E  S  E  B  B  M
T  G  T  O  W  G  D  E  S  M  D  A  K  O  V
B  G  S  L  S  J  O  P  L  N  P  N  T  O  R
U  A  E  H  I  U  E  M  Z  U  P  Z  O  A  I
Q  H  D  G  F  S  R  I  T  S  E  S  J  P  C
```

ANNIHILATE	BLOCK	CATASTROPHE
CONSIDER	DESTROY	DISASTER
DURABLE	HAGGLE	IMPEDE
PONDER	QUARREL	ROBUST

Let's Compose Sentences

Look back at the definitions and example sentences. Can you write a sentence for each of the words?

Haggle:

Ponder:

Annihilate:

Catastrophe:

Impede:

Robust:

My Notes

Word Search Solutions

Puzzle 1

ADEQUATE	AFFILIATION	ALLOCATE
CONDOR	INDIFFERENT	LIBEL
PREFERENCE	PREY	RELATIONSHIP
REPUTATION	RESOURCES	SUITABLE

Puzzle 2

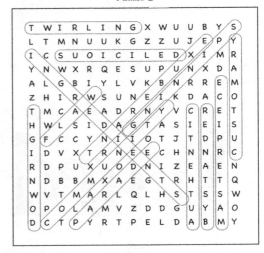

AUTHENTIC	BYSTANDER	COMMUNITY
CUSTOMARY	DELICIOUS	DOWNRIGHT
EXUBERANT	FLAW	INGREDIENTS
MASTERPIECE	PARADE	SPINNING
TWIRLING		

Puzzle 3

AGITATE	CONNECTION	FORMIDABLE
IMPRESSIVE	INTIMIDATE	LIAISON
MANDATORY	NECESSARY	ON TIME
PUNCTUAL	SCARED	WORRIED

Puzzle 4

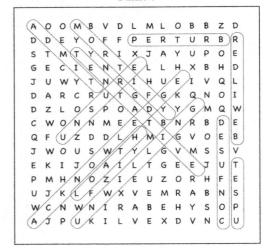

ACKNOWLEDGE	ADMIT	BEWILDER
CONFUSED	LOATH	MORTIFY
PERTURB	TENTATIVE	UNSURE
UNWILLING	UPSET	

Puzzle 5

CANNY	DESIRE	LARGE
NIMBLE	OPINION	QUICK
RESPOND	RETORT	SHREWD
SUBSTANTIAL	VIEWPOINT	WHIM

Puzzle 6

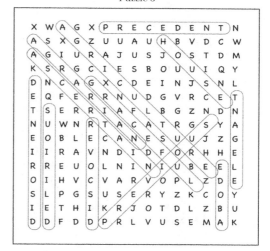

ABODE	AGRARIAN	AGRICULTURE
ASCERTAIN	DELIRIOUS	DISCOVER
DISORIENTED	ELEGANT	GRACEFUL
HOUSE	PRECEDENT	PREVIOUS

Puzzle 7

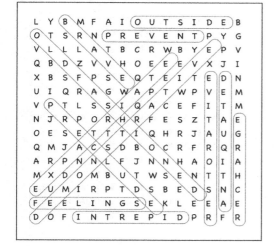

ANTIQUATED	BRAVE	DEMONSTRATIVE
EXPATRIATE	FEELINGS	INTREPID
OLD FASHIONED	OUTSIDE	PRECLUDE
PREVENT	RECHARGE	RESTORATIVE

Puzzle 8

ADDICT	ANTAGONIZE	COMPARE
COMPETENT	COMPONENT	CONTRAST
DEVIOUS	HOSTILE	SEVERAL
SKILLED	UNTRUSTWORTHY	

Puzzle 9

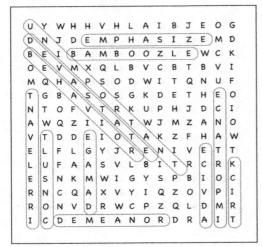

ADVICE	BAMBOOZLE	BEHAVIOR
CONSULT	DAMAGE	DEMEANOR
DEVASTATE	EMPHASIZE	IMPORTANCE
IRRELEVANT	TRICK	UNIMPORTANT

Puzzle 10

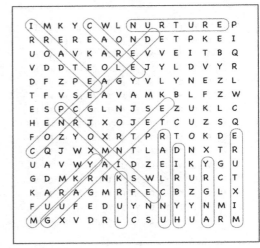

ANGRY	CARE	CONCEALED
GUARANTEE	HYBRID	IRATE
LURK	MIXTURE	MURKY
NURTURE	PROMISE	UNCLEAR

Puzzle 11

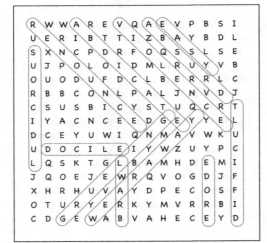

ABDICATE	ABSURD	BRAWL
DIFFICULT	DOCILE	EASY
ERODE	GRUELING	LUDICROUS
RENOUNCE	VIOLENCE	WEAR AWAY

Puzzle 12

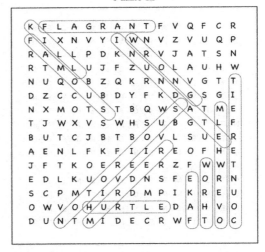

COUNTERFEIT	FAKE	FAMOUS
FLAGRANT	HURTLE	INUNDATE
KILL	MURDER	NOTORIOUS
OVERWHELM	THROW	WRONG

Puzzle 13

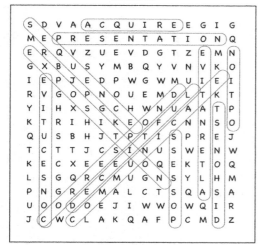

ACQUIRE	ALTERNATIVE	COMMUNICATE
CONSECUTIVE	CORRESPOND	DECEITFUL
DISHONEST	EXPOSITION	OPTION
POSSESS	PRESENTATION	SEQUENCE

Puzzle 14

ATTRIBUTE	BOYCOTT	CALCULATION
CHARACTERISTIC	DAWDLE	DIVERSITY
ESTIMATE	FAMISHED	HUNGRY
PROTEST	VARIETY	WASTE TIME

Puzzle 15

BEG	DESPONDENT	DISCOURAGE
DISHEARTEN	FLABBERGASTED	FUNNY
HILARIOUS	HOPELESS	IMPLORE
MAGNITUDE	SCALE	SURPRISED

Puzzle 16

BEFORE	ENSUE	FADE
FAIR	FOLLOW	HARDWORKING
IMPARTIAL	INCREDULOUS	INDUSTRIOUS
PRIOR	RECEDE	

Puzzle 17

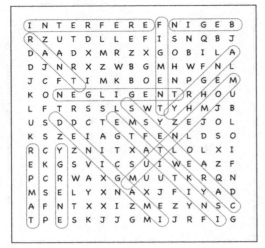

ANGRY	BEGIN	CARELESS
ENERGY	FIGMENT	IMAGINED
INITIATE	INTERFERE	MOMENTUM
NEGLIGENT	RANT	TAMPER

Puzzle 18

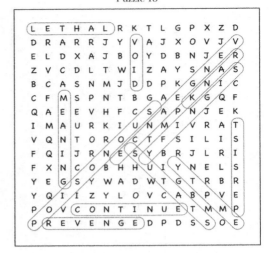

CONTINUE	EMPTY	LETHAL
MEANING	PERSIST	POISONOUS
RANK	REVENGE	SIGNIFY
STATUS	VENGEANCE	VOID

Puzzle 19

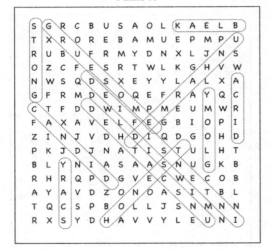

ACRID	BLEAK	CANDID
GLOOMY	GRUESOME	HONEST
INTENSIFIED	SCARY	STRONG
UNHARMED	UNSCATHED	

Puzzle 20

ANNIHILATE	BLOCK	CATASTROPHE
CONSIDER	DESTROY	DISASTER
DURABLE	HAGGLE	IMPEDE
PONDER	QUARREL	ROBUST

Ace your Spelling and Vocabulary Skills Further!

Scan code with your phone.

Available on Amazon

Made in the USA
Monee, IL
27 June 2024